Zen For Beginners

Finding Your Inner Peace and Joy Through Zen Concepts, Meditation and Practices

Garland P. Brackins

Zen For Beginners

Bluesource And Friends

This book is brought to you by Bluesource And Friends, a happy book publishing company.

Our motto is **"Happiness Within Pages"**
We promise to deliver amazing value to readers with our books.
We also appreciate honest book reviews from our readers.

Connect with us on our Facebook page www.facebook.com/bluesourceandfriends and stay tuned to our latest book promotions and free giveaways.

Don't forget to claim your FREE books!

Brain Teasers:
https://tinyurl.com/karenbrainteasers

Harry Potter Trivia:
https://tinyurl.com/wizardworldtrivia

Sherlock Puzzle Book (Volume 2)
https://tinyurl.com/Sherlockpuzzlebook2

Also check out our best seller books

"67 Lateral Thinking Puzzles"

https://tinyurl.com/thinkingandriddles

"Rookstorm Online Saga"

https://tinyurl.com/rookstorm

Table of Contents

Introduction

Chapter 1: What is Zen?

Chapter 2: Why Meditate in Zen?

   How Zen Will Help You

   Why Zen Over Other Practices

Chapter 3: Zen Meditation Techniques

   Your Zen Environment

   Positioning Yourself
      Half Lotus Position
      Full Lotus Position
      If You Have Mobility Issues

   Breath Work

   Developing A Routine

Chapter 4: Zen Teachings

   Lesson 1: Avoid Dogma

   Lesson 2: Keep Your Beliefs in Perspective

   Lesson 3: Choose For Yourself

Lesson 4: Be One With Your Suffering

Lesson 5: Learn What Real Happiness Is

Lesson 6: Experience Anger, Don't Become It

Lesson 7: Be Present

Lesson 8: Listen Without Judgment

Lesson 9: Become Aware of Your Words

Lesson 10: Maintain A Peaceful Community

Lesson 11: Be Aware of Injustices

Lesson 12: Become Peace

Lesson 13: Be Gentle and Kind

Lesson 14: Respect Your Sexuality

Chapter 5: Slowing Down

Chapter 6: Gaining Mindfulness

Sight

Smell

Touch

Taste

Zen For Beginners

Sound

Awareness

Conclusion

Introduction

Congratulations on downloading *Zen For Beginners!*

In the mainstream spiritual community, "Zen" has become somewhat of a buzzword. Many new age millennials use Zen to describe a state of being. While that holds true, many fail to realize that Zen is actually a structured form of meditational practice that is meant to bring value to a person's life. As you will learn about in this book, Zen is a Japanese school of training which teaches that a certain state of being is accomplished through meditation and practice. Because it has very real roots and a very real structure, it is a good reason for you to follow the ancient Japanese teachings to achieve real Zen in your life.

If you are ready to discover what Zen truly is, how it is achieved and how you can begin using this method of meditation and mindfulness in your life, then it's time to dive in! Do not be afraid to take your time and absorb the lessons of Zen as you learn about this powerful ancient practice that can change your life, just as it has changed many before yours. And of course, enjoy!

Chapter 1: What is Zen?

Zen is a combination of something that we are, and something that we do. Zen is a disciplined practice that we achieve by realizing the joy of being, which allows us to be Zen while also doing Zen things. Although Zen is a fairly specific teaching, it is not one that someone must convert to or choose over anything else in order for them to achieve. Instead, Zen is a universal practice that anyone from any walk of life can gain benefits from. When it comes to developing and becoming Zen, there is no dogma or doctrine that you must follow to actually achieve Zen. Instead, Zen is something that is achieved by stepping into the ultimate or absolute reality, but without stepping away from the ordinary or relative lifestyles that we have grown used to living. Experiencing Zen is our birthright - everyone can achieve Zen simply through choosing to.

Zen For Beginners

Buddhism was brought to Asia from East India, and was readily adopted by the vast majority of the population due to it being an accommodating and flexible belief system. It was through Buddhism that the concept of realization was taught to the masses, and then Zen was introduced by the Japanese Buddhists who decided that the state of being needed an official name. For thousands of years, Zen has been the accepted name of the state of being and doing. It has become more deeply understood as thousands of people have come to educate themselves on Zen teachings.

Zen is said to be achieved through a dedicated and consistent meditation practice that allows one to regularly come into a state of realizing the non-duality of the world. In other words, separately we are individuals, and together we are one, meaning that we are both one apart and one together. The conditioned and the unconditional may exist together in unison, and it is possible to understand and experience both of these states through a consistent meditation practice.

When it comes to understanding Zen, it is important to understand that what you are learning about is not a religion but is, instead, a practice. There is no reason to make a big deal about it, or to feel the need to identify it, or even to shift your religious beliefs to embody the art of Zen. Instead, you can simply become and experience Zen by choosing to integrate this practice into whatever existing practices you already have.

Stepping into Zen requires you to stop attempting to understand life through an intellectual approach, and instead becoming aware that what exists out there is far vaster than the rational mind can comprehend. By tuning into the present moment and tapping into a present state of awareness, one can achieve Zen. In other words, you can flow with the vastness of all, knowing more than you could possibly know, while simultaneously knowing nothing at all. You become plugged into the flow of life, embodying and embracing all that is and trusting that while you are are plugged into it, you are not inherently required to know all of it. What matters is that you have access to it all.

This simple yet profound practice of Zen can support you in removing yourself from the weight of the past and the future, as well as from any self-imposed prisons or barriers that you have established between yourself and others. Instead of being isolated, separated, or trapped in any moment beyond the present, you can begin using Zen meditations to connect to the present moment and enjoy your life for what it truly is. You can also begin releasing the constructs that you have built around your mind as the result of past burdens and future worries, so that you can live freely in the moment, without fear of what has already happened or what has yet to come.

As you continue practicing Zen, you will find that extending your mind and growing into a larger version of yourself becomes inevitable. Your mind will continue to grow and develop as you come to recognize your "self" and your experience as being far greater than the constraints you have around yourself to date. As a result, you will become more open, unhindered, flowing, and far more confident.

Chapter 2: Why Meditate in Zen?

Zen is a powerful practice that can enable you to become more present, mindful, and available to experience the life before you. The idea behind Zen is that you only live in the now, which means no longer holding yourself against the burdens of the past or worrying about the development of the future. Ideally, when you are no longer burdened by your past, the past hurts that prevented you from feeling safe enough to trust or bold enough to try will no longer impact you, thus enabling you to remain free-spirited and open to what life has to offer. When you are no longer worried by your future, you stop acting rigidly and you open yourself up to the possibility that the future may be beautiful and enjoyable.

Beyond allowing you to exist in the present moment, Zen offers plenty of other great benefits as well. In this chapter, you are going to discover what Zen has to offer and why it is an ideal meditation practice, as well as why you might consider Zen over other meditation practices that are available to support you with your growth in life. This way, you can understand what it is that you are seeking to develop, and why Zen may be the most optimal meditation practice for you to achieve it.

How Zen Will Help You

Zen is helpful on many different layers of mental practices. When you choose to begin using Zen meditation practices, you will discover that your capacity to enjoy a freer mindset increases. Many people who use Zen practices find that they are freed of their tendency toward anxious behaviors because they are no longer living in fear of what might happen in their lives. Instead of falsely believing that your future is destined to be overwhelming, too much to handle, or bad in one way or another, you open yourself up to believing that you are capable of enjoying a wonderful life. Perhaps bad things may happen, but you also open yourself up to the fact that good things may happen too. You also begin to realize that, more often than not, neither bad things nor good things happen, as life is frequently filled with neutral events that fill the space between the good and the bad. Your awareness of this space between the good and the bad allows you to begin realizing how simple and enjoyable life is, rather than leading you to always measure your life by the bigger experiences that you may have exclusively paid attention to in the past.

Another great benefit of Zen practices is that Zen is actually a very versatile practice that can be used on a day-to-day schedule. You are not required to do anything elaborate or excessive in order to engage in Zen. You can easily awaken to daily Zen practices so that you can increase your overall meditation and mindfulness practice. For those who are looking to enjoy a flexible and manageable meditation practice, Zen is a great opportunity for you to begin incorporating mindfulness into your life instead of feeling burdened by a massive schedule.

As you begin to discover yourself through Zen and you come to learn more about who you are, you also learn how to cultivate compassion for yourself and for those around you. Mindfulness has a powerful capacity to help you begin seeing things from a new perspective, which allows you to understand more of what life has to offer and how you can tap into the value of life itself. As you continue tapping into these newer and higher perspectives, it becomes easier for you to see life beyond your own vantage point and instead begin understanding life from many different angles. As a result, you can see life from other people's perspectives, which makes it easier for you to have more compassion for yourself and for those around you. Believe it or not, this increased compassion will also support you in having an easier time forgiving others, making it easier for you to heal yourself.

Zen For Beginners

The increased perspective of Zen meditation also enables you to begin identifying your true path to happiness. Your capacity to see beyond what you have already been seeing enables you to step away from emotional attachment to your current path, which may include suffering, so that you can begin looking into new paths that may bring greater joy. As you pursue your path of true joy from your higher self through meditation, you come to understand that your life is not about money, power, success or status, but instead, it is about true happiness. It is likely that these other elements will exist in your life as you develop it, yet they will not be the primary thing that you are focusing on any longer. You will come to learn that money, success, power, and status can all be developed in a way that brings significantly less suffering, thus enabling you to have a far more enjoyable lifestyle.

Because of your changed perspective, Zen will also support you in understanding that what truly makes you happy likely lies beyond consumerism. As a result, you begin to consume less as you start to realize that what will bring you true joy is far more than just your material belongings and that which money can buy. Instead, happiness comes more from your collective experiences and your life from moment-to-moment, not from the belongings that you purchase and hoard. Because of this change, you will likely find yourself stepping away from consumerism behaviors so that you can begin enjoying a more real and wholesome lifestyle. In addition to no longer consuming things through purchasing, you may also find that your consumerism tendencies in general begin to ease up. For example, if you previously watched large amounts of television and found yourself constantly engrossed in television shows for hours on end, you may find that you no longer wish to watch such large quantities of television.

Zen For Beginners

As you begin spending more time alone outside of the consumerism bubble, you find that you begin discovering your true nature. When you no longer spend time consuming so much content and products from the consumerism society, it becomes easier for you to discover who you truly are. This is because the less time you spend engaging in consumerism, the more time you have to engage in other behaviors, allowing you to enjoy life in a way that is truer to who you are. You will discover that, instead of sitting and watching hours of television, you may gain more joy from learning a new craft, sport, or hobby that allows you to work more with your hands and exercise your intellectual mind. You may discover that you enjoy spending more time in meditation, or simply walking around your local neighborhood, or even just slowing down to enjoy the moments of your life that previously rushed by in a blur. These things that you may not have paid attention to or made time for in the past begin to become more meaningful to you as you awaken to your Zen state of consciousness.

As these new things increase in importance to you, you also begin to discover who you truly are. Spending more time in nature may have you realizing that you are a gentler and more compassionate soul than you originally believed yourself to be. Spending more time doing needlepoint crafts or painting may have you discovering that you are more intuitive and creative than you thought yourself to be. The more you engage in what you are creating in your day-to-day life, the more you will learn about your own character, strength, and preferences.

Releasing yourself from the standard lifestyle of modern society also provides you with the capacity to simplify your life. As you are no longer engaging in the mad dash toward the latest trends and status symbols, you can begin enjoying a life that is far more easygoing and simpler in nature. You may find that in the past you needed more and more excitement to experience true joy, whereas now you can experience it simply by slowing down to watch the sunset or watching your children play in the park. The things that you did not notice before become significant again and you find yourself enjoying life on a far deeper level than you allowed for in the past. As a result, you begin enjoying a far simpler lifestyle that can encourage you to experience all that life has to offer. While you will still want to engage in and enjoy the larger excitements in life, such as amusement parks and fancy vacations, you will also begin engaging in and enjoying the smaller excitements in life, like a well-cooked breakfast or a unique-looking flower.

Why Zen Over Other Practices

There are many types of practices out there that you can look to in order to help you begin experiencing a more present and mindful state of awareness in your life. These days, you can find mindfulness meditations all over the internet that are intended to help you release from the stresses of life so that you can engage more deeply in the present moment. Many of these meditations are powerful, and will provide you with great benefits, too. The key difference here is that Zen practices allow you to not only study for mindfulness and meditation, but also opens you to an entire philosophy of thought that allows you to truly embrace mindfulness in your everyday life.

Many other mindfulness practices will have you carving out time for mindfulness throughout the day, which supports you with your ability to become mindful in the moment. You may even have certain practices that you are to try and engage in throughout the day so that you can begin enjoying a degree of mindfulness throughout the day. However, oftentimes, these one-off practices are not designed to truly give you the full understanding of what mindfulness is and how it can be used in every moment of every day so that you can experience an entirely new way of thinking and existing. When you begin to study the Zen philosophy, you not only come to understand how to do Zen practices and incorporate Zen into your life, but also how you can become Zen. This means that as you continue embodying the Zen practices, you can begin noticing that throughout your day-to-day life, you are more mindful and intentional than you were prior to your practice. As a result, not only do you experience relief from symptoms of anxiety, depression, stress, angst, or other overwhelming emotions in the moment, but you also experience an ongoing improvement over time.

Chapter 3: Zen Meditation Techniques

When you begin engaging in Zen meditations, you are going to want to do so by getting into the right position and engaging in the proper breathing patterns. These two elements are necessary for you to begin experiencing full Zen in your meditational practices. In this chapter, you are going to understand how you can begin incorporating posture and breathing into your meditation practice so that you can begin experiencing the energy of Zen. You are also going to discover how you can develop your own meditation routine so that you can regularly revisit and nourish your Zen state.

Meditation is a key element in Zen practices, as it is where you begin to connect to the energy of Zen and know what it truly feels like. When you engage in Zen energy through meditation, it becomes easier for you to know what Zen feels like so that you can consciously and intentionally tap into a state of Zen energy throughout the day. The more you meditate and connect with the energy of Zen, the more familiar your body and mind becomes with this state of awareness, which makes it easier for you to achieve it over time. For that reason, you will always want to have a steady and powerful Zen meditation practice to rely on as you continue developing your Zen over time. Your meditation practice will not only help you develop your Zen state, but it will also help you begin to maintain it so that you can continue connecting to this energy state over time. That way, you are always able to continue cultivating and living within a Zen flow.

Your Zen Environment

Taking care of your physical surroundings is an essential part of creating a comfortable environment for you to achieve a Zen state in. You need to have an environment that will be free of distractions, is comfortable, welcoming, and safe for you to experience peace and quiet in. While you can certainly do this by heading into a quiet room and simply getting started, you will have a better experience if you put some thought and effort into developing the right environment for you to begin meditating in.

Ideally, you should be meditating in the same spot every single day so that your meditation space becomes a sanctuary to you. Because you are going to be meditating in the same space each day, do not worry if your space requires time for you to be able to develop it and really turn it into the right space for you. Start simply, and allow your space to grow over time as you begin decorating it with everything that feels right for you. You can start decorating using a low-light lamp, sea shells, candles, stones, flowers, art work, or anything else that helps you to feel at peace in your environment. Do not be afraid to customize this space to make it your own, as you truly want this space to be a haven as you meditate and allow yourself to explore the world of Zen in your sanctuary.

In addition to things that will remain in your environment long term, such as decor, you should also consider things that you will bring into the environment each time you meditate to create a comfortable space for yourself. For example, you may wish to light candles, burn incense, or listen to music so that you can begin to feel an even deeper state of relaxation while you meditate. You may also wish to use a meditation pillow, anointing oil, essential oils, or other sensory tools that you can use to relax your senses. The more you can relax your entire body and mind, the more peace you are going to feel from within, which will allow you to achieve a deeper state of Zen.

Lastly, when you begin your meditation, you will want to consider your physical body itself. Whenever you meditate, seek to eliminate or minimize wearing any jewelry and wear loose fitting clothing to support you in feeling more relaxed. Wearing anything tight or that has too many different embellishments can be uncomfortable, and may prevent you from being able to relax. Further, make sure that you dress appropriate to the temperature of your space, as you do not want to begin feeling extremely hot or cold as you attempt to relax completely in your meditation practice.

Positioning Yourself

Once you have cultivated the right environment for your Zen experience, the second step in achieving a Zen state is having the right position for you to be able to effectively achieve Zen. Your body is going to need to be positioned in such a way where it feels comfortable, open, and relaxed. This ensures that you have an easier time feeling calm and connected to the present moment. While there are many ways that you can likely position yourself to feel relaxed, Zen meditation requires you to be seated. Zazen, or the art of "doing" Zen, literally translates to "seated meditation," so it is only natural that you will need to be seated in order to fulfill this meditation experience.

When it comes to Zen meditation, you want to be seated with your legs crossed in front of you, your back straight, and the crown of your head drawn up toward the ceiling. You also want to gently relax your hands on your thighs or knees, typically with your palms facing upward. It is very important that you keep your spine straight, so if you need to use a meditation pillow to achieve this straightened back, do not be afraid to incorporate one into your meditation. If you do use a meditation pillow, sit upon it with your legs off of the edge, as this will help add more height to your bottom, creating an easier space for you to elongate your spine.

Zen meditation positions have two typical postures: the half Lotus Position, or the full Lotus Position. If you are not particularly flexible and you are new to

Zen meditation, you will want to use the half Lotus Position. If you are more flexible or you have been doing Zen meditation for a while and are ready to advance your practice, you can begin working toward creating and meditating in the full Lotus Position. Both positions are described below.

Once you have chosen the right position, make sure that you relax your head and keep it comfortable. You can achieve this by keeping your neck aligned with your spine so that your head stays straight, which will minimize any pressure or discomfort that you may feel around your spine. If you are having a hard time aligning your neck with your spine, you can tuck your chin in slightly to further elongate your spine and keep your neck straight. Imagine that you have a line running through your spine and up and out your neck, and allow that line to pull your neck straighter so that everything rests comfortably.

After you have allowed your body to sink into the right position, go through and check all of your smaller muscles. Relax your jaw, tongue, and cheeks. Keep all of your face, head, and neck muscles completely relaxed. Loosen your shoulders, drop them down, and allow the rest of your body to relax as well. Consciously scan through your entire body and intentionally release any tension or pressure you may be feeling throughout your body to ensure that you are not holding onto any stressors that may cause discomfort or distract your meditation later.

Half Lotus Position

The half Lotus Position is done by sitting in a fairly standard cross-legged position. You want to have your left foot on top of your right thigh, and your right leg under your left thigh.

Full Lotus Position

The full Lotus Position is done by sitting with one foot on top of each opposite thigh, as you sit in a cross legged position.

If You Have Mobility Issues

If you have mobility issues, or you find that either of the Lotus Positions is uncomfortable, you will not want to use either of these poses. Your meditation pose should never bring you pain nor discomfort, as this can distract from your meditation and may also cause further damages that can leave you feeling even less relaxed. Instead, you might consider sitting on a chair with your spine straight and your feet planted firmly into the floor, or even laying down on your back with your spine straight if you are unable to sit well. You can always modify your position to serve your needs if your physical mobility is ailed, so do not feel as though you have to avoid Zen meditation if you are unable to achieve a half Lotus Position or full Lotus Position.

Breath Work

The next step in achieving your Zen state is allowing yourself to begin the meditation practice, which will commence with some intentional rhythmic breathing exercises. The first breathing practice you are going to work with is focusing on breathing in and out through your nose so that you can begin to feel the warm and cool sensations of your breath as it continues to move through your nostrils. Nasal breaths can help bring your awareness into your body, which can make it easier for you to follow your own natural rhythm as you meditate.

As you continue breathing, begin focusing deeply on your breath and feeling the sensations. As you are meditating, notice your breath as much as possible. Pay attention to the air outside of your nose, the air that comes through your nose, the air in your throat and lungs, and the air as it is released once again. Notice as many different sensations associated with your breath as you possibly can, as this helps bring you centered into your body and grounded into the present experience. Any time you find yourself becoming distracted by something else, allow yourself to become aware of your breath once again. Rather than trying to distract yourself or scold yourself for allowing your mind to wander, simply encourage your awareness to come back to your breath and let these distracting thoughts naturally subside on their own. Observe your thoughts without judgment and without trying to change them, and instead simply accept them for what they are - just thoughts.

As you continue breathing, decide what you want to do with your eyes. There is no right or wrong answer; you may keep your eyes open, let them fall relaxed, or you can close them. Choosing to consciously position your eyes in a way that feels right for you can allow you to stop worrying about whether or not you are doing the right thing and instead start focusing on your breath so that you can feel at peace.

The next step in rhythmic breathing is to start sinking deeper into an actual rhythm. You can do this by slowly elongating each breath, allowing yourself to breathe in for an extra moment or two, and breathe out for an extra moment or two. Remain controlled and gentle in your breathing, as you do not want to begin breathing so heavily that you find yourself needing to breathe through your mouth, as this will create discomfort within your body. Ideally, you should be steadily breathing in to the count of eight and out to the count of eight, as this is a comfortable rhythm that will keep plenty of oxygen flowing through your lungs. Do not hold your breath on the inhale or exhale like you might with other meditations, but instead allow the breath to continue to flow freely in a way that feels right for you.

Developing A Routine

Now that you are aware of how your meditation practice should look like, you can begin to develop a routine that will allow you to meditate more consistently. As you continue meditating, entering a state of Zen will become easier for you, meaning that you can meditate longer and experience more significant benefits from each meditation session. That being said, developing a consistent practice will require you to keep yourself continually practicing so that your mind, body, emotions, and spirit all become used to entering a state of Zen.

You can develop your practice in a few different ways. First, you want to do so by keeping your routine consistent every single day so that you know exactly what to expect at any time you begin meditating. Creating a consistent routine is going to support your mind in creating a pattern that allows you to identify when meditation practice starts, so that it is easier for you to enter a deeper and more consistent state of meditation. So, if you start your meditation practice each time by lighting your candles and turning on low music, make sure that you start your practice this way every single time so that your mind and body know exactly what to expect.

You also want to develop your routine by looking at it as a long-term investment of your time and attention, rather than something immediate and final. Do not be afraid to build up to your ideal practice and let yourself evolve over time, as this is going to support you in creating a practice that is truly yours. If you want to start with just two minutes of meditation per day and you only turn the lights low and sit on a pillow because that is all you have to start with, do not be afraid to start there! Over time, you can start adding more decorations or tools to your space to use to create a tranquil energy while also stretching your practice out over a longer period of time. Follow the pace that feels right and natural for you, and trust that your natural progression will be plenty to help you teach your body to engage in meditation and get the most out of it.

One thing that is important after every meditation session as you are building a routine, and even after you have completed your routine, is self-reflection. Reflecting on the meditation that you have enjoyed and feeling into the parts that you felt you did right and the parts that you would like to improve on is important. Learning how to reflect upon yourself will support you with increasing your mindfulness and self-awareness, while also supporting you in improving your practice so that you can gain even more benefits from it over time. You might even consider keeping a journal and writing down how each meditational experience was so that you can begin allowing yourself to recognize where your improvements are and where you can improve even more. This can also be a wonderful tool to help you release any thoughts or emotions that may arise from your meditation practices so that you can continue to keep your energy free flowing and comfortable.

Chapter 4: Zen Teachings

Zen is not only a style of meditation, but it is also a school of philosophy based on certain thoughts or beliefs about life itself. This is why many people falsely believe that Zen is religious in nature: It does carry with it plenty of wise teachings that have been passed down from some of the earliest Zen Buddhist monks. These teachings are not so much a necessary guideline for people to follow, as a school of thought or a set of orders that were discovered by individuals as they meditated.

In this chapter, we are going to explore 14 pieces of wisdom passed down by Zen Buddhists so that you can develop a deeper understanding for what Zen truly is, how it impacts your life, and how you can get the most out of this practice. If you really want to take your own Zen practices to the next level, it is a good idea to have a journal that you can write about these topics in, as you may find yourself pondering what they mean and how they can assist you in your life. Spending time considering and learning to understand these teachings for all that they have to offer is a powerful way to really embody all that Zen is, and take your own Zen experiences to an even deeper level.

Lesson 1: Avoid Dogma

Be aware of any rules that attempt to solidify themselves as concrete and final. In our society, we are raised to believe that there is only one thing to aspire to and that there is only one right way to achieve that and it creates suffering on many different levels. Do not be afraid to see rules as guidelines and to make your own when you find that the ones being fed to you by society or by certain members of society are ill-fitting to your dreams. You can reduce a significant amount of suffering by letting yourself off of the hook when it comes to living up to other people's expectations of who and what you should do with your life.

Lesson 2: Keep Your Beliefs in Perspective

We have a tendency to create beliefs or perspectives about the world and then hold tightly to them, to the point where we become deeply attached to these beliefs or perspectives. In reality, beliefs and perspectives are malleable and can be changed as we learn new information or discover that they are no longer supporting us in living a fulfilling life. Do not be afraid to loosen your grip on your current beliefs and perspectives so that you can allow yourself to have more creative freedom and expression when it comes to living your life.

Lesson 3: Choose For Yourself

We cannot force others to think the way we do, nor can we force ourselves to think the way that they do. Not even our relatives can think on the same level that we do, and it would be ignorant to believe that they could. Attempting to make other people think like we do, or attempting to think like they do, only leads to suffering as we attempt to minimize or eliminate unique experiences. You can certainly have compassion and empathy for others, as well as receive compassion and empathy from others, but do not attempt to foster someone else's school of thought or vice versa. Respect the differences that exist in your opinions and learn to be at peace with the fact that you may never think the same way.

Lesson 4: Be One With Your Suffering

When we attempt to run away from our own suffering, we only create more suffering. Learning how to sit with, feel, and work through your suffering is a powerful opportunity for you to begin releasing it so that you are no longer attached to your suffering. In our society, we have a tendency to try and push suffering away by "fixing" it. Instead, we should be identifying, studying, analyzing, and learning to understand our suffering, and simply allowing it to exist. This way, your suffering will no longer have any power over you..

Lesson 5: Learn What Real Happiness Is

Modern society has a very misconstrued idea about what happiness is and how it can be achieved. Most often, it is believed that happiness will be achieved when you have a high paying job, a nice car, 2.5 kids, a house with a white picket fence, and neighbors who come over for afternoon barbecues. In reality, nearly no one's life looks like that, and anyone who does have a life that looks this way is still dealing with their own suffering. Release yourself from what you have been taught happiness is, and instead start looking into what happiness truly is. You will likely discover that happiness is truly inner peace, reliability, freedom, and compassion. These are the only things that can bring you true, sustained happiness.

Lesson 6: Experience Anger, Don't Become It

Emotional maturity or emotional intelligence is a powerful tool that you can use to start detaching from your intense emotions like anger, so that you can begin experiencing them rather than becoming them. When you find yourself experiencing anger, allow yourself to recognize it as an experience. Feel it rising in your body, notice what sensations or thoughts come with it, and do not be afraid to sit with it and ask it what exactly it is aspiring to achieve at that moment. The more you spend time sitting with your anger and learning to understand it, the more you are going to be able to experience anger rather than become anger. This means that, when the experience is over, you can resume your contented state and release your attachment to the anger itself, rather than holding on to it longer than necessary.

Lesson 7: Be Present

There is a famous Buddhist saying, "If you are depressed, you are living in the past; if you are anxious, you are living in the future." When it comes to Zen teachings and Zen meditation, your goal is to release yourself from both of these points so that you can begin experiencing the present, where you have the capacity to cultivate peace with whatever your present circumstances may be. The more you can detach from the past and future and instead stay connected to the present moment, the easier it will be for you to experience peace and contentment.

Lesson 8: Listen Without Judgment

Learning to listen to those who are speaking without judging what they are saying, either with positive or negative judgments, is a powerful skill to educate yourself on. As you learn how to increase Zen in your life, teach yourself how you can begin listening without judgment by detaching to the personal meanings of what people are saying to you. Instead of listening and associating someone's opinions or stories with your own personal opinions, simply accept them for what they are. Practice unconditional love and acceptance as you listen to people, and watch how your communication styles and relationships change.

Lesson 9: Become Aware of Your Words

In addition to becoming aware of what other people are saying, you also need to become aware of what you are saying to others. Words are our most powerful tools, and using your words appropriately is a necessary skill to learn if you are going to allow yourself to reduce your suffering in your own life. If you are speaking carelessly, it becomes easier for you to say things that you do not mean, or to speak in a way that comes across much harsher than intended. Learning how to communicate effectively means that you can always say exactly what you mean, and with the right intentions. This way, you do not say things that you will come to regret, thus creating unnecessary suffering.

Lesson 10: Maintain A Peaceful Community

Learning how to maintain a peaceful community, or maintaining peace between yourself and others, is important. A very important Zen teaching discusses on the importance of bringing your Zen energy from your meditation into the world around you so that other people can experience your Zen for what it is, too. When you practice Zen, look for ways that you can start bringing this energy into your community by sharing greater acts of kindness with those around you. Rather than going through life with a stern or vacant look on your face, look at the people around you and share the moment with them, and even share a friendly smile. Experience people as they are, even if they are just passersby on the street, and notice what a different it makes in the energy of your own world and in the energy of others.

Lesson 11: Be Aware of Injustices

As you begin generating more peace in your community by becoming and behaving in alignment with peaceful energies, also make sure that you are remaining aware of injustices. Pay attention to anything in the community that is not fair, and do not be afraid to act if you can in order to minimize the injustices being experienced by the people in your community. If you notice a man on the sidewalk begging for change, for example, do not be afraid to stop and support this man in any way that you can to avoid him being forgotten about or harmed due to his lack of change. If you see a woman with children on the bus in need of a seat, do not be afraid to stand up and offer her a seat or find space for her to sit down so that she can relax. Often, the smallest acts are the most profound, so do not feel like you have to give away everything you have to create justice for others. This would end up creating an injustice for yourself. Look for opportunities to create a fair community for everyone, so that everyone can live in peace and comfort with you in this community. The more you spread peace this way, the more peaceful your community will become.

Lesson 12: Become Peace

Learn how to really embody peace in your life, and make a point of learning how to spread peace around at every opportunity that you have. Spread peace and prevent violence by learning how to be the balanced, sovereign energy that can comfort a room and keep everyone relaxed in any situation. This is less about learning to emotionally manage others and taking their energy on as your own, and more about learning how to become a peaceful mediator in the world around you. Do all that you can to become a peaceful mediator and to truly become peace so that you can spread this peace into the world around you. The more we become peace, the more we can spread peace, and as a result the more we can heal the world through the spreading of peace.

Lesson 13: Be Gentle and Kind

You always need to agree to be gentle and kind with yourself and others as you work to protect the general well-being of everything that coexists on our planet. Always seek to be generous and respectful of that which belongs to others, while also working toward preventing those who profit from suffering. Learn how you can minimize suffering in the world by being gentle and kind with yourself and others, and learn how to do it in all ways. Be gentle and kind with healing, with your behaviors, with your voice, and with your intentions as you walk the Earth. You will find that your life becomes a lot more peaceful and significantly less suffering is experienced when you seek to become more gentle and kind.

Lesson 14: Respect Your Sexuality

The final lesson is that you need to learn how you can respect your sexuality. Having sex with people just for the sake of it should be avoided, as sex is a sacred act that should only be shared between two people who truly care about one another. It is important that you begin educating yourself on how sacred sex is, and only sharing it with other people who view it as an equally sacred art. Do not have sex because you are lonely, bored, or because you feel like it, as this will only create needless suffering. As well, always respect others' right to their bodies and their sexual desires, and never attempt to harm anyone for your own sexual gain. Instead, preserve your vital energies for self-realization, and do everything that you can to prevent sexual abuse.

Chapter 5: Slowing Down

As you may be picking up on by now, Zen teachings are about learning how to slow down so that you can begin enjoying more of life itself. Learning how to truly slow down, not just physically but also mentally, emotionally, and spiritually can allow you to both increase your peace while also minimize your suffering, as you are detached from the world around you. When it comes to embodying Zen in your life, learning how to slow down will enable you to begin moving your Zen practices from your meditation space to your actual life.

Slowing down can occur in all areas of your life, so it is important that you seek to learn how you can embody the art of slowing down in as many ways as possible. You can begin embodying the art of slowing down from morning through to bedtime, and every moment in between if you truly pay attention. Of course, there will be periods of time in your life where hectic energies arise and you are no longer paying attention to slowing down; yet the more you set the intention of slowing down, the more consistently you will be able to achieve this state.

As you continue your meditation practice and continue drawing your awareness to your need to slow down and enjoy yourself, you will begin to recognize where you can start slowing down even more in your life. You should look at any element of slowing down as a positive sign, as slowing down even just a small amount each day can be life changing. The more you slow down and recognize your ability to do so, the more you will be able to slow down over time, which will eventually lead to you being able to completely step aside from a busy go-go-go-type lifestyle and stop and enjoy your life as it happens.

Zen For Beginners

To inspire you to slow down, let us look at the many different parts of your day that you can infuse with slowness, and what you can gain from taking these moments of slowness so that you can see the value that slowing down truly has to offer.

Imagine you were to wake up in the morning, and instead of rushing out of bed and into the bathroom as you normally would, you paused for a moment and noticed the sunshine coming through the curtains. Consider how it would feel to spend just a moment or two breathing and watching the light dance off the wall as you allow yourself to feel each part of your body awakening. Perhaps instead of jumping out of bed, you might stretch first, increasing the warm and fuzzy sensations pulsing through your body as you awaken to the energy around you. Then, you gradually get out of bed and as you do you notice the ground beneath your feet, and the beautiful belongings that you have selectively placed around your space. If you have a partner or someone you live with, maybe you can pause for a moment and notice their presence, and give thanks for them being there. Then, you head off for the bathroom to get started for the day ahead.

All throughout your morning routine, you have this same slowed-down experience. You feel the shower water pouring down over your body, taste your coffee and eggs, and experience the sensation of minty fresh toothpaste cleansing your mouth. You spend a few moments enjoying the silence before the hustle and bustle of the day, or maybe you spend a few moments breathing in the warm energy of your family as they all get ready for their own day activities. You take your time dressing and you dress in something that makes you look and feel great, allowing you to feel even more excited for your day.

When you arrive at work, rather than feeling the immediate overwhelm of your duties, you instead breathe through it and allow yourself to go moment by moment. Your ability to slow down and experience each task not only increases your productivity, but also reduces your stress, meaning that you are working better and you feel better doing it. Your nagging coworkers or bosses do not upset you at this time, as you are feeling peaceful and relaxed, and you do not feel the need to overreact to them.

At lunch time, you slow down and breathe for a few moments, and you allow yourself to taste your lunch. Instead of working through lunch, you take that time and enjoy your lunch, chewing through each bite and savoring the flavors that you experience as you eat. You also slow down to savor the drink that you are enjoying, allowing yourself to feel refreshed and fulfilled from your drink. Spend a few minutes after you are done eating, digesting and allowing yourself to feel settled, so that your body does not feel shocked or nauseous from you rushing into action right away. Allow your digestive processes to complete.

Later, when you are done working, take your time in driving home and pay attention to all of the traffic signs that you typically miss due to being so used to the drive. Slow down and notice the sky, the people passing you by, and the other cars on the road so that you can experience yourself as well as everyone else surrounding you. Listen to the music on the radio, or listen to the road outside as you turn the music off to change the experience up for once. Allow yourself to become present in the moment so that you can experience the drive that you typically do not pay attention to any longer out of habit.

At home, slow down and enjoy your alone time, your friends, or your family. Put your phone down and sink into each moment, allowing yourself to experience everything that it has to offer. Challenge yourself to drink in every experience from every moment so that you can feel the fullness of what your life has to offer. If you notice yourself checking out, breathe in deeply and bring yourself back into the moment so that you can experience it once again. As you continue learning how to breathe in the moment and bring yourself into it, becoming present will get easier, and you will find that your days become far more enjoyable and fulfilling. Rather than only noticing the parts of your life that stand out from the routine, you can start noticing all of the moments of your life. This way, the days will stop blending together and creating feelings of overwhelm and overlap and will instead start feeling like full, enjoyable experiences.

Chapter 6: Gaining Mindfulness

Slowness is part of creating mindfulness, but if you truly want to live a Zen life and experience mindfulness, you are going to also need to focus on the art of mindfulness itself. The difference between these two acts is that slowing down simply means no longer rushing through life, and mindfulness means truly tapping into each experience and getting all that you can out of it. Mindfulness is about slowing down to drink in the experience as well, although if you truly want to become mindful, you will do it through activating as many of your senses as you can with each experience, and directing your thoughts to stay clearly focused on the present moment.

There are many points throughout your day where you can become mindful, and you can also carve out mindfulness breaks to allow yourself to intentionally come back into your body and start experiencing mindfulness all over again. In the previous chapter, you were walked through a day where you had the capacity to identify numerous points where you might begin experiencing mindfulness, such as by watching a light on the wall or paying more attention to the surroundings on your drive home. In this chapter, rather than showing you periods of your day where mindfulness can come into play, we are instead going to identify how you can draw on each of your five senses and your conscious awareness into the present moment, so that you can achieve a deeper level of mindfulness.

Sight

You can draw your sight into your mindfulness practice by regularly paying attention to the things within your realm of vision with the intention of gaining as much information from them as you can through your vision. Since your vision is likely one of your most used senses, learning how to use your vision to increase your mindfulness practice can be highly valuable. You can use your vision to draw regular mindfulness moments into your day by stopping to look at your surroundings and creating a story or message in your mind about what you are looking at. For example, if you are in your office, you might tell yourself about what office supplies and decorations you are surrounded by, what colors they are, and what they are made of. Ideally, you want to cognitively become aware of as much information as you can regarding an item, solely through your visual experience with it.

Smell

Often, we are surrounded by a wide variety of smells, even though we rarely pay attention to them unless there is something particularly outstanding about a smell around us, such as one that is particularly gross or one that is yummy. If you want to become more mindful, every now and again, stop and ask yourself about the scents that you are presently being surrounded by, and begin drawing as much information from them as you can. Notice what they smell like, what they remind you of, where they are coming from, how they make you feel, and any other pieces of information that you can draw from these scents.

Touch

Every day we are touching things, and again we are rarely registering what information we are gaining through our sense of touch. We become unaware of the sensation of the door handles we turn, the clothes we are wearing, or the seats we are sitting in unless something stands out to us and draws our awareness in. Instead of waiting for something different to occur, begin becoming aware of your surroundings and the sensations that you are physically feeling in your surroundings on a more consistent basis. Notice what is touching your skin, what the temperature of the room is like, and how you physically feel in any given moment, and allow yourself to become mindful of what that experience is like.

Taste

Taste may be one of our lesser-used senses, as we typically do not engage with taste unless we are eating something. A great way to use taste to develop a mindfulness practice is to begin seeing every single food item and beverage as an opportunity to become mindful. Instead of guzzling your drinks or eating food quickly, slow down and start becoming aware of every sip or bite. Notice what the sensation of those food items feels like in your mouth, what flavors you gain from them, and whether or not you genuinely enjoy them. Pay attention to the textures and sounds as you chew, and what it feels like as you swallow the food. Enjoy each bite or drink, and allow all of your eating and drinking experiences to become daily mindfulness moments.

Sound

Noise pollution is a real thing, and it has caused many of us to become desensitized to the sounds around us. We become so used to sounds like the typing of a keyboard, the sound of air vents or cars on the road, such that we stop hearing them altogether because our brain no longer registers them as important. The truth is, these are all a great opportunity for you to become mindful and to check in with your surroundings. If you slow down and give yourself a moment to listen to all of the sounds happening around you, you allow yourself to check into your environment and begin experiencing it more mindfully. This type of awareness can be a huge plus in helping you tune back into your environment.

Awareness

Awareness is not necessarily a sense, but it is a very important tool when it comes to experiencing and developing mindfulness. You can develop your awareness by simply noticing what you are thinking and where you are focusing, and choosing to direct that awareness toward anything that feels right for you. You may direct it toward specific thoughts, the task at hand, solving a problem, engaging in the present moment, or simply even relaxing more. There is plenty that you can do with your awareness, so do not be afraid to regularly check in and notice where you are directing your awareness so that you can consciously and intentionally direct it somewhere more effective.

Conclusion

Congratulations on completing *Zen for Beginners*!

I hope that this book educated you on the ancient art and practice of Zen, and how Zen can help you change your life by bringing in more peace into your experiences. From understanding what Zen is and where it comes from, to developing your own routine and understanding the philosophy behind the practice, I hope that you have gained greater knowledge and understanding about this practice. This way, you can start creating your own Zen practice and feel a deeper sense of connection and peace within your own life.

The next step after reading this book is cultivating your own Zen meditation practice so that you can begin feeling a deeper sense of peace in your own life. Remember, it is okay to start where you are at and to allow your practice to develop over time; you are not required to start off perfectly. Even if you are just starting with sunlight and a small pillow on the floor as you meditate for two minutes, trust that this is plenty. Over time, you will begin to meditate longer as your space becomes more comfortable and personal, and you will have an easier time bringing Zen into your everyday life. Be patient, gentle, and kind. Have trust that you are doing the right thing at all times.

Lastly, if you enjoyed this book, I ask that you please rate it on Amazon Kindle. Your honest feedback would be greatly appreciated.

Thank you.

Garland P. Brackins

Zen For Beginners

Connect with us on our Facebook page www.facebook.com/bluesourceandfriends and stay tuned to our latest book promotions and free giveaways.

Printed in Great Britain
by Amazon